EMERGENCY QUESTIONS

RICHARD HERRING

© Richard Herring, 2017
Published by Go Faster Stripe Ltd
21 Hanover Street, Canton, Cardiff CF5 1LS
www.gofasterstripe.com

We are not just books - we are mostly DVDs in fact.

ISBN: 978-0-9560901-6-4
Catalogue No.: GFS-84

Publication Design: Stefhan Caddick
Proof reading: Ben Evans
Printed by PCP, Port Talbot

EMERGENCY QUESTIONS

RICHARD HERRING

CONTENTS

THE INTRODUCTION

Welcome to the wonderful and bewildering world of Emergency Questions.

It contains five hundred questions, but this is not a quiz book and there are no definitive answers (though I chuck in a couple just for fun), though there are definitely some that are funnier than others. You or your friends must provide the replies, but no one can tell you that you are right or wrong. Or rather that you are correct or incorrect. Some of the questions might reveal that you are wrong in the head. But that's part of the fun.

Emergency Questions originated in my Internet interview show, *Richard Herring's Leicester Square Theatre Podcast*. In fact, as it turned out, the very first question I asked Tim Minchin in the very first episode, "Have you ever tried to suck your own cock?" became one of the main EQs (as no one calls them) of the first few series. It wasn't that I was particularly anxious to find that out about Tim, I'd just been doing some stand up about auto-fellatio and it seemed the natural thing to ask. Like pretty much everything in this podcast nothing was planned.

I think EQs (it's catching on) really started to develop when I interviewed Jonathan Ross in an early podcast. He had been a bit of a last minute booking and I hadn't prepared as much as I should have and I was also somewhat in awe about having got a proper person off of the telly on to my stupid homemade show. I wanted to impress Ross, maybe hoping he'd have me as a guest on his proper show (he never did, but did book the other guest on that week's show, Francesca Martinez) or just respect me as a fellow interviewer. But I was floundering and got to a point where I genuinely couldn't think of a single thing to ask him or even to say. I didn't even remember to ask him if he'd ever tried to suck his own cock and by all accounts he has quite an impressive member, so that was a terrible oversight.

I realised I needed some definite things to say if my brain ever froze like this again, or if there was a bit of a lull from the guest or even if we just needed to lighten the mood.

It was a total accident, but the *Emergency Questions* (I tried with the EQ thing but it just wasn't me) became a vital part of the podcast. Not just because they provided catchphrases for the regular listeners or because they dug me out of a hole, but because they had a weird way of making the guests open up.

I have done many interviews as the interviewee and they are usually pretty dull, repetitive and samey. Someone has briefly researched you by looking you up on Wikipedia or just ask you the three most obvious things that you can ask a comedian (Where do you get your crazy ideas from? What do you prefer – live comedy or TV (sometimes radio or writing)? What is your favourite joke?) Like me, all my guests have answered such questions so many times that now they are more or less working from a script. But if you ask them a question they've never been asked or one that surprises them, they are forced to use a different part of their brain. Comedians want to entertain, so even if you ask them a dull question like, *Have you ever tried sushi?* then they will try and come up with a story. And if it's a question they've not been asked before then chances are it will be a new story or one they've never thought to tell. Or if you just get them to access the creative part of their head, you will find that the subsequent answers they give might be more open or emotive or just funny.

So suddenly asking Stephen Fry what it is like to be Stephen Fry (a question that came not from me, but a Welsh schoolboy who I employed in my Cardiff question mine) can open a door that will mean he tells you. With searing honesty.

But I don't think the *Emergency Questions* only work when asked to comedians or other assorted celebrities. In fact I know they provide a diverting parlour game for many people. Sometimes more than that. One listener told me that he had spent an hour, trapped in a chalet on the side of a mountain after being caught up in an avalanche asking his friends about ham hands and talcum powder dispensing nipples. It took their mind off possible impending death until thankfully they were rescued (but who knows how many other groups of friends have played them, only not to be saved and have thus spent their last hour on earth debating time travelling fingers? It's almost certainly millions). But others have asked them to friends or strangers or on dates (a bit of a risk with some of the fruitier ones, but then, hey, if someone is prepared to tell you about the time they tried to suck their own cock on a first date then they're almost certainly a keeper).

You can use this book as a solo amusement, or try out the questions on friends or enemies, at a dinner party or to a stranger on a bus or if you have your own interview show and you've asked all the stuff from off of Wikipedia, lob a couple of these babies in. Quite a few people seem to have taken the opportunity to ask the ham hand/sun cream armpit question in newspaper Q and A's or their own interviews with celebrities. Jodie Foster, for example went for the sun cream because her kids are ginger and she didn't like wasting time getting the unguent from a bottle (google "Jodie Foster ham hand" to see it).

Anyway, sit back in your high-backed armchair, open a packet of arguably-not-as-good-as-they-once-were Kettle crisps and use your finger to travel through time (or turn the pages, which is similar) whilst nibbling on your other hand and imagining it's made out of ham (which it more or less is), take the phone off the hook so no six foot tall penis men can ring you and ask you for a date and enjoy these emergency questions.

1. Have you ever tried to suck your own cock?

2. Which would you prefer? A hand made out of ham or an armpit that dispensed suncream?

    N.B. The hand would grow back each time you ate it and would function perfectly as a hand, though would leave a greasy residue on everything it touched. The sun cream would be of a factor of your choosing and be enough for your own personal use, but you would not make enough to bottle and sell.

3. If you had to have sex with an animal – if you *had* to – what animal would you have sex with and why?

    Rich says: "I'd choose the okapi. From behind it looks like a lady wearing zebra print trousers and it's also got a surprisingly long tongue. If I had to I mean. If I had to."

4. What would it take for you to fellate the actor Keith Allen?

5. What age were you breast-fed until?

6. Have you ever seen a ghost?

    N.B. Interesting fact for after the question has been answered – ghosts do not exist. Anyone who says they have seen one is thus mentally imbalanced.

7. Have you ever seen a Bigfoot?

N.B. If someone starts telling you about the time they saw a Sasquatch or a Yeti, immediately stop them talking. The question is "Have you ever seen a Bigfoot?" Also if someone says they've seen a big foot you are allowed to punch then in the face and legally there is nothing they can do about it.

8. If you had to have sex with a monster from Dr Who – if you *had* to – which of his many foes would you choose?

Rich says: "I'd go for that liquorice allsort monster from rubbish Sylvester McCoy era, because after making love you'd have a delicious snack."

9. What is your favourite cheese?

Rich says: "Sorry to my home town, but no question, it's haloumi. Any other answer is incorrect."

10. Has your sibling ever seen a ghost?

11. Who is your favourite historical character?

Rich says: "Mine is the pretender to the English throne, Perkin Warbeck."

12. What is love anyway?

Subsidiary question: Does anybody love anybody anyway?

13. Would you rather have the attributes of a radiator or a fridge-freezer?

14. What do you think happens when we die?

Rich says: "I believe whatever you believe will happen to you when you die, that's what happens. Which is an organisational nightmare for God. He has to knock up new Heavens every five minutes, based on the whim of lunatics."

15. What's it like being *(insert name of the person you're asking)*?

N.B. Watch out! This one seems pretty innocuous but can make people reveal emotional secrets that nobody was aware of. If you're wondering what it's like being Richard Herring – fucking ace, ta. But I never learned to read – see!

16. Would you rather have a hand made out of suncream or an armpit that dispensed ham?

17. If you could choose one thing for your armpit to dispense, what would that thing be?

18. Have you ever put anything up your urethra?

19. What is the meaning of life?

N.B. Whatever they say, you must say, "the answer is that there is no meaning. Suck it up biatches."

20. What is the chemical composition of a carrot?

N.B. Polyacetylenes can be found in **Apiaceae** vegetables like carrots where they show **cytotoxic** activities. **Falcarinol** and **falcarindiol** (cis-heptadeca-1,9-diene-4,6-diyne-3,8-diol) are such compounds. This latter compound shows antifungal activity towards **Mycocentrospora acerina** and **Cladosporium cladosporioides Falcarindiol** is the main compound responsible for bitterness in carrots.

Other compounds such as **pyrrolidine** (present in the leaves), **6-hydroxymellein**, **6-methoxymellein**, **eugenin**, 2,4,5-trimethoxybenzaldehyde (**gazarin**) or (Z)-3-acetoxy-heptadeca-1,9-diene-4,6-diin-8-ol (**falcarindiol 3-acetate**) can also be found in carrot.

21. Would you rather be a cow or a badger?

Rich says: "Reveals a surprising amount about whether a person prefers conformity or freedom. Or being milked or gassed by farmers."

22. Have you ever seen a famous TV animal in real life?

23. Have you ever tried to communicate with the dead?

24. If you had to marry a Muppet – if you *had* to – which Muppet would you marry?

Rich says: "Janice from the band."

25. Have you ever had a near death experience?

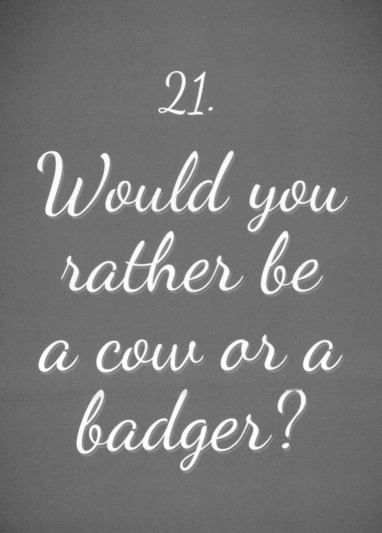

21.

Would you rather be a cow or a badger?

26. Are you a ghost?

27. What's so funny about peace, love and understanding?

Rich says: "They are intrinsically silly, especially when someone tries to imply that they're not"

28. Would you rather have a tit that dispenses talcum powder or a finger that can travel through time? What would you do with such a power?

N.B. You would produce limitless talcum powder so could sell it for profit. Only your finger travels through time. You'd be able to look through the hole to see what was going on, but only your finger could interact.

29. If you got on Dragon's Den, what product would you pitch?

Rich says: "I'd pitch a hair gel that transformed into shampoo when you got into the shower – it would not be activated by rain though. Somehow."

30. What's the worst experience you've ever had in a hotel?

Rich says: "In a Travelodge in Cambridge I found someone else's bogey on my shower curtain."

31. Which celebrity would you like to stroke your hair as you die?

Rich says: "I think I chose Bouncer from Neighbours. Or Goldie from Blue Peter. I don't know why."

32. Do you have a favourite towel? What is your best story about it?

Rich says: "I do. It's Old Bluey. Portly comedian Andre Vincent once borrowed it without asking when he stayed in our flat in Edinburgh and I've never been able to enjoy using it again."

33. What is your most mundane encounter with a celebrity?

Rich says: "One of the blokes who used to be in Hollyoaks and I think is now in Casualty and might be married to Topsy and Tim's mum in real life once said hello to me thinking he knew me, but then realised he'd just seen me on TV."

34. How sensitive are your nipples?

N.B. Take a chance – if you're on a date, make that the first question you ask. Don't even say hello.

35. Who would win in a fight, CJ from Eggheads or Jeremy Corbyn?

N.B. You must formulate a reasoned response even if many years have past and you are not clear who these celebrities are.

36. What really killed the dinosaurs?

37. Would you rather date a man who was a six foot tall penis or a man who instead of having a penis had a tiny man?

N.B. The six foot penis would have a face on his helmet, but otherwise is just a huge penis (without balls). He would be wearing a suit jacket with false arms on it to give himself a more human appearance. The tiny man would be living, with his feet implanted in his host man, but be a separate individual with his own personality. He in turn would have a tiny man instead of a penis and so on to infinity.

38. King Herod never killed any children. Discuss. Please quote sources.

Rich says: "It's weird that the only source that mentions his slaughter of the newborns is the New Testament. You'd think other historians would have mentioned that. Also he died in 4BC, which is a clue."

39. Have you ever come up with an idea for conceptual or performance art that you think is better than any of the guff that gets nominated for the Turner Prize?

Rich says: "Walk a Mile in my Shoes – every pair of shoes a person ever owned in their life, from cradle to grave, stuck to the floor along a promenade a mile long. Also Me1 vs Me2 Snooker."

40. Are you ever mistaken for a celebrity? Which one?

Rich says: "Hideous motorcycle freak Charley Boorman. Ironically he genuinely advertises Herring Shoes and I think he only got the gig because they thought he was me."

41. Do you have any good ideas for terrorist atrocities?

Rich says: "Explosives in Berocca form that you can just add to water on the aircraft. Or boob bombs. I have loads of these. I am prepared to sell to the highest bidder."

42. Who would be your Desert Island Dicks? That is, which eight Richards would you take with you to a desert island? You get Richard Herring as your Shakespeare Richard.

Rich says: "Bacon, Briers, Mayall, Richard II, O'Brien, Osman, Pryor and I might try to sneak in Richmal Crompton for sex."

43. If I got turned into a turkey right now, what would you do?

N.B. This is a question that a young Sofie Hagen asked her teen idols, Westlife. They did not answer it very well.

44. Why can't everyone be babies?

45. If Alan Sugar asked you to name his autobiography, what would you call it?

Rich says: "I Remind Me of Me at That Age"
"Firing Blanks"
"Ass-poo full of Sugar" (only works if he secretly suffers from rectal diabetes).

46. Have you ever had the opportunity to assassinate a public figure?

Rich says: "Yes, Michael Gove. At least twice. My apologies for the failure to do so."

47. Does sex with a robot count as cheating on your partner?

Rich says: "No."

Rich's wife says: "Yes."

48. Have you ever put your genitals in or near the mouth of a dead animal?

Follow up question: "A living animal?"

49. Which is worse: bestiality or necrophilia?

50. What crimes have you got away with?

51. Have you ever flown a kite?

52. What is the worst emergency you've ever
been involved in?

Rich says: "When I worked on an American summer camp in 1986,
on the last day there was a massive fire which consumed the forest
we were in and blew up gas tanks. We were 50 miles from the
nearest fire station. I thought I would die. I think I might have. Maybe
I am a ghost."

53. What song would you like to replace the
national anthem?

Rich says: "Do the Hucklebuck."

54. Kettle crisps are not as nice as they once were.
Have I changed or have they? DON'T LET
THEM ANSWER THAT. IT IS RHETORICAL.
If you could travel back in time to compare any
food of today with an equivalent of the past
     a)   what time?
     b)   which food?

55. If you had to go on a week's holiday with a
Spitting Image puppet – if you *had* to – which
would you choose?

N.B. Bear in mind that the puppet would choose the holiday
destination and that the puppeteer and voice over artist would also
come with you but you could not communicate with them directly,
only as the puppet.

Is sex with a Ghost Cheating?

56. Sport is intrinsically stupid. Discuss.

N.B. Do not be tempted to turn this into a joke question by saying Discus instead of discuss. It isn't funny. And this is a serious question. Although I am not sure it actually counts as a question, because it's not technically a question.

57. Is sex with a ghost cheating?

58. Why do elephants have such low rates of cancer? 5% vs 25% of humans.

Rich says: "It's because they have 20 TP53 genes to humans' one. It's like a smoke detector for cancer."

59. Can you name another animal which is cancer resistant?

Rich says: "The naked mole rat – though some cases have recently occurred in this disgusting creature."

60. Should penis transplants ever be allowed? What are the possible terrifying consequences of such a procedure in your opinion?

Rich says: "I just fear that a rich man will harvest my beautiful penis for his own use before I have finished with it."

61. What's your worst experience with the delivery company Yodel?

62. Would you rather date a woman who was a six foot vulva or a woman who instead of having genitalia had another woman living in a burrow between her legs?

63. What's the best museum you've ever been to?
Rich says: "Keswick's Pencil Museum."

64. If you could murder one person and have an 87% chance of getting away with it, who would you kill?

65. What is the biggest animal that has bitten you?

66. Have you got what it takes to be a spy?
Rich says: "I find it hard to keep secrets, so I would be a great double agent. Until I went back into the office of the spies that I was supposedly working for and immediately told them of my subterfuge."

67. Is Dutch a genuine language or are the people of Holland just taking the piss out of us all?
Rich says: "It is definitely made up. I don't know how they communicate when no one is looking but it's definitely not in Dutch."

68. If you could jump into a pool of something, what would it be?

69. What age would you like to be when you get to Heaven, presuming there is a Heaven and you get to choose what age you'll be up there?

N.B. I am not asking what age you will die, just what age you'd like to revert to when you are walking/flying around in Heaven. Also what age you should choose what age you'll be, because it will vary a lot.

70. If you could get a law named after you, what would it be?

Rich says: Herring's Law is that whatever locker you choose at the gym, when you come back to it, the person in the next door locker will be there getting their stuff in or out and in your way.

71. If you could have a part of the human body named after you what would it be?

Rich says: I would like the external meatus (what kids at my school used to offensively call "The Jap's Eye") renamed as the Herring's Eye.

72. What do you consider your median achievement?

73. Do you ever worry that you have already lived your life and are now in a care home with Alzheimer's Disease and what you perceive as reality is just a distorted memory of the first time this happened?

74. Is there anything purple within 10 feet of you?

75. Which five celebrities are on your celebrity shag list?

N.B. This is a list that you and your partner decide it will be OK for you to have sex with in the unlikely event that the opportunity arises.

Rich says: "Gemma Chan, Rebecca from Cbeebies, Robert the Robot from Justin's House, Anne Widdecombe and Metal Mickey."

76. Have you ever tried sushi?

77. Have you ever tried sashimi?

78. Who is your favourite mythological figure?

79. Have you ever demolished a wall or a building?

80. What's the worst incorrect rumour you have heard about yourself?

Rich says: "That I invite women back to my hotel room and make them dance, whilst I sit in a high-backed armchair and masturbate. I have never done this and anyone who says I have is lying."

81. Would you rather have a tongue that could taste impending danger or get a free iPhone?

82. Why do we have frozen peas? Why is that the only vegetable that the principal way we use it is in frozen form? I know there are other frozen veg, but only the pea is principally used as a frozen, rather than fresh or tinned commodity.

    Why?

83. Have you ever been in the vicinity of a bigfoot, but not seen it, but sensed it watching you?

84. If you had to have sex with an item of food – if you *had* to – which food would you choose? Do you think it would be morally wrong to eat the food after you had made love with it? Or unhygienic at least?

85. Where do you stand on transubstantiation?

86. Would you rather have the ability to shoot bees out of your eyes or have a pair of shoes that never needed to be cleaned or repaired?

87. If you could communicate with one animal, which animal would you communicate with and what would you ask them?

88. If you were given the powers of a King Midas, what would you turn everything you touched into?

Rich says: "I would make everything I touched turn into the thing that it already was, but it was now holding or covered in diamonds which I would then be given. Of course once I had the diamonds they would turn into more diamonds with diamonds on them, but I wouldn't be too bothered by that."

89. How many fingers was Richard Herring holding up as he first asked this question?

Rich says: "It was three."

90. If you had the powers of a Gary Sparrow and could travel from the 1990s to the 1940s what would you do?

91. Have you ever been to Barometer World?

92. Would you like to live in a world where everyone else was barometers?

93. How did the murder of Thomas A Beckett affect Anglo-Papal relations in the 12th Century?

Rich says: "Well let's just say it didn't help."

94. Do you know the way to San Jose?

Rich says: "Not from here, no."

95. There is no such thing as morality. Discuss.

Rich says: "Again, is this a question? That can be the question."

96. Which RHLSTP guest would you most like to snog and why?

Rich says: "Limmy, because he looks so normal"

97. I once burped during the minute's silence at the Ascension Day Service – what was the most audacious thing you did whilst at school?

98. Do you think it's possible that Postman Pat has had some kind of breakdown and the people of Greendale are just putting up with him out of some kind of misplaced loyalty to his younger self?

99. Would you rather do a Freaky Friday/Vice Versa with Brian Blessed or CJ from Eggheads?

N.B. You would be back to yourself after the day was over and would not be culpable for any crimes you had pretended to commit or lies about going to Mars.

100. Which conspiracy theory do you think might actually be true? Come on, one of them must be. And the others were just made up to make that one look just as crazy.

Rich says: "I think Paul McCartney was replaced by a lookalike with slightly different ears in the 1960s."

101. Have things turned out like you expected them to?

102. Do you think the Tim Allen film, "The Santa Clause" could ever happen in real life? If you were press-ganged into being Santa would you feel happy or resentful?

103. If you had to dig up the corpse of a celebrity who died in 2016 and have sex with it – if you *had* to – which one would you choose?

Rich says: "The guy who played Barry on Hi-di I li. In a way, I think it's what he would have wanted."

104. Would you prefer to be a lion for day or a lamb for a lifetime?

105. How do you sleep at night?

106. What do you consider to be the most mediocre chocolate bar?

Rich says: "Definitely Twix. It is nobody's favourite or least favourite snack."

107. What is the most unconvincing lie you have ever told?

108. Would you be willing to eat a bowl of crickets for $40,000?

N.B. This very specific question comes from buzzkenya.com. It sounds like they might be willing to pay you that exact amount it you do.

109. What happened to Lazarus the second time he died?

110. If a serial killer kills another serial killer does that work like conkers?

111. What is your favourite keyboard shortcut?

112. Would you prefer to live in an igloo or have to dance the fandango every day at 9pm for the rest of your life?

113. Would you rather have no ears or no dignity?

108.

Would you be willing to eat a bowl of crickets for $40,000?

114. If you had to would you rather give up chocolate or cheese? If you *had* to.

115. If you had the power to bring down planes with your mind, would you be able to resist doing so just once? Just to check you really could? Or would you do it loads anyway, laughing at the destruction you had wrought?

116. What's the strangest thing you ever found in your junk email?

117. What is the most embarrassing thing you've ever tried to squeeze down the drain in a shower?

118. Would you prefer to have a superpower which allowed you to predict the next day's weather with 75% accuracy or be able to assess if food past its sell-by date was still safe to eat?

119. If you could choose which liquid you weed, what liquid would you wee?

N.B. It can still be wee if you wish. Bear in mind you will probably die quite quickly if the urine inside you is not expelled.

120. What modern day item do you think will seem ridiculously archaic in 10 years time?

121. If you had the ability to rearrange your internal organs into the configuration of your choice, what changes would you make?

122. If you were in a Groundhog Day situation what would be the worst crime that you would commit, knowing that when you woke up, it would almost certainly not have happened?

123. If you had to bathe in excrement – if you *had* to – what animal or individual human's excrement would you choose to bathe in?

124. If you were given the ability to fluently speak another language (that you can't currently speak) which language would you choose and why?

125. If you were God what flavour would you have made ejaculant? Because it's like God didn't even consider that people were going to eat it.

126. Do you ever worry that you are a character in a computer game, operated by some bored teenage deity or alien who is deliberately just making loads of shit happen to see what you'll do, like you're nothing more than an ant under a microscope and that soon he will be bored and have you killed in a ridiculous way? Because I do.

127. If you had to be killed in a natural disaster – if you *had* to – which natural disaster would you choose?

   Rich says: "If I HAD to, I would be killed in a Vesuvius like volcanic explosion and try and get in a funny pose so that I'd make future archaeologists laugh when they made a plaster cast statue from the gap I left in the ash."

128. Can you think of any situation in which a pussy should be grabbed?

129. Why do fools fall in love with Darren Day?

130. Is there actually a person of whom you'd be prepared to drink their bath water? Who is it? What if they had a really pooey bum that day?

131. **What walks on four legs in the morning?**

Rich says: "Acceptable answers include a horse, an okapi, a dog."

132. **Did you ever see a lassie go this way and that?**

133. **What is the most impressive celebrity that ever came to your school?**

Rich says: "Rick Buckler, the drummer from the Jam, was the brother of our art teacher and he once played in our school hall with his arguably less successful band Time UK."

134. **Did any future celebrities go to your school?**

Rich says: "Jack Bessant, the bassist from Reef."

135. **Did any siblings of celebrities teach at your school?**

Rich says: "Yes, Mr Buckler, the art teacher was the brother of Rick Buckler from the Jam. I said that two questions ago. Why aren't you paying attention?"

136. **What is your preferred epithet for male genitalia?**

Rich says: "The honourable member for Fuckinghamshire."

137. How long do you think it would take you to write 500 emergency questions?

    Rich says: "What am I up to? 137? What the fuck? I don't think it's possible to do 500. Why did I say I could? Do the questions in this answer count? No? That sucks."

138. Did you ever learn to juggle? If so how many things can you juggle? I demand to see proof of your juggling claims.

139. If I could guarantee you would be unkillable, indestructible and uninjurable for the next ten years, but would die once the decade was up, would you go for it?

140. Could you ever have sex with someone that calls breasts "boobies"? What if they did it while you were having sex? Would you stop having sex with them?

    Rich says: "I would definitely stop. I don't mind if someone calls them boobs though. It's weird."

141. If you had to murder one person at your work/ college/family - if you *had* to - which person would you murder?

142. If you didn't have to murder one person at your work/college/family, but knew you could get away with it, which person would you murder?

143. What makes a good emergency question?
Rich says: "That's a good question."

144. If you had to put everyone called Smith in a league table based on their worth who would be:
> a) *the best Smith*
> b) *the median Smith* and
> c) *the worst Smith?*

Only answer when you can give a name for all three Smiths.

145. When you have fears that you may cease to be before your pen has gleaned your teeming brain, what do you do?
Rich says: "Write stuff down more quickly."

146. Have you ever had a dream that seemed so real you thought that it was true? How do you know it wasn't and that this is just a dream?

147. What's your favourite drink? If you found out it was actually made out of wasp urine and always had been, would it still be your favourite and would you carry on drinking it?

148. Would you rather be immune from ever getting chlamydia or have free KitKats for life? (You would get 365 four finger Kitkats per year, or 366 on a Leap Year, but would still be able to get chlamydia).

149. If you could go into the transportation chamber from "The Fly" with a living creature of your choice, which creature would you choose?

    Rich says: "An okapi, as long as I got to be the human top half and the okapi bottom half, like a sexy okapi centaur."

150. What was your nickname at school?

    Rich says: "TK Junior. My dad, TK Herring, was the headmaster of the school and commonly known as TK."

151. If you were a little pig, what would you make your house of in order to deter the big bad wolf?

    Rich says: "I would make my house out of fire. Wolves are scared of fire. Also I would be nice and warm. And there would be a lovely smell of bacon."

152. If you could have a sex robot of any human living or dead, who would you have a sex robot of?

N.B. Even if the person is dead the sex robot will be "alive".

Rich says: "I would have a sex robot of my wife, so that I could still have sex with her even when she is away… Has my wife stopped reading this now? Good. It would be Gemma Chan."

153. Who would win in a fight between the shark from Jaws and Jaws from James Bond?

154. If you had a silo what would you store in it?

Rich says: "Baked beans. So I could always eat baked beans."

155. International Women's Day?
When's International Men's Day?

Rich says: "November 19th."

156. Are we all doomed or is there some way out of this mess?

157. Would you rather wear a hat made out of beef or shoes made out of yoghurt?

N.B. The yoghurt would be usual viscous consistency and the beef would rot over the course of time and attract vermin and vultures.

158. If you got the chance would you cryogenically freeze yourself at the point of death in the hope of being cured in the future? How do you think you'd fit in if it worked out for you? Wouldn't you be worried the future humans would think you were a primitive idiot?

159. What's the most pretentious book you've ever bought, but never read?

160. Is less more? Or is it less? And more is more? I mean occasionally less is better than more, but that wasn't the question was it? It's always less.

161. If everyone else in the world left in a spaceship and left you behind, so everything belonged to you: Where would you live? What paintings would you have on your wall? Would you be lonely? Where would be the most ostentatious place you would masturbate?

162. Do you think anyone will actually count up all the questions in this book to check that there are definitely 500?

  Rich says: "I am certain of it. Some idiot will. Will you really be that idiot? Apparently that doesn't count as another question. Are we seriously only up to 162 now?"

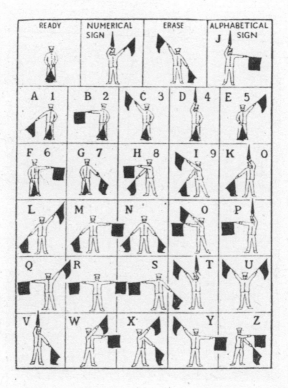

163. Would you rather be a sparrow or a snail?

164. Are you the postman or the letterbox?

165. What is your favourite colour?

    Rich says: "Whatever they say pretend to consult a chart and then say, 'That means you're a psychopath.'"

166. What is more important: your job or your family? And why?

    Rich says: "Like Jim Carrey and Adam Sandler in all their films I used to think my job was more important, but now I realise it is family. Then again I am neglecting my family to write 500 emergency questions for a very small amount of people who like my work, so what does that say about me? Also I have to keep working or my family will die, so it's a facile question."

167. Is the glass half full or half empty? And what does it say about you if you are too afraid to ask someone out straight if they are an optimist or a pessimist and instead have to use a confusing glass metaphor? You haven't even said what's in the glass. What if it's a glass of poison? You've learned nothing about us but we have learned a lot about you.

168. Do you think that the Adam Sandler film "The Cobbler" could ever happen in real life?

N.B. If the person answering the question hasn't seen "The Cobbler" then please make them watch "The Cobbler" before they answer. They must watch the whole of it and you must spend the whole time looking at their face, to see how they are reacting. Then ask them again.

169. If you were Adam Sandler how would you even begin to spend the millions of dollars you made for appearing in "The Cobbler"?

Rich says: "I would build a silo and fill it with baked beans so that I never had to buy food again."

170. Do you make a mental file of answers that would work well if you were ever on Pointless?

Rich says: "Of course, doesn't everyone. If you get Kevin Spacey films then say 'Heartburn.'"

171. When you're watching films how much time do you end up Googling the actors to find out if they are still alive?

172. Have you ever been in a canoe?

173. What do you think the chances are of me accidentally repeating a question in this book?

174. Have you ever had a dream that accurately predicted the future?

175. Do you secretly wonder if you are the new Jesus? Maybe you are.

176. Would an eternity in Heaven actually be Hell for you?

    Rich says: "Hmmmm, deep... No."

177. What is the most embarrassing thing that you have done for sexual gratification?

178. You know when you wake up in the middle of the night with a feeling of inexplicable existential dread, you're not sure why you're so panicked, but it feels like life is meaningless and terrible and pointless... what if that's the only time you have any kind of mental clarity?

179. What is your favourite pinball table?

    Rich says: "If the answer is anything but "Addams' Family Pinball" then you are WRONG. If your answer is "What's a pinball table?" then all your future answers are void."

180. Have you ever crossed paths with a serial killer?

181. Did you ever go camping with your family? What are your abiding memories of that awful experience?

Rich says: "I fancied a Dutch girl called Carla and snogged with her after I had accidentally fallen into the lake in the dark. It was the best experience of my life. I touched her boobs."

182. Which is best, Cheddar Caves or Wookey Hole?

Rich says: "Cheddar Caves is the correct answer, even though Wookey Hole is objectively better."

183. If you had to do a Human Centipede with two other people – if you *had* to – and you were in the middle, which two people and at which end would they each go?

Rich says: "I would like my mouth attached to Gemma Chan's anus and my anus attached to Michael Gove's mouth. That way no one has to put their lips on Michael Gove's anus – something that has, as yet, never happened and never should. Also Gemma Chan's poop would almost certainly be delicious, but its deliciousness would have been sullied by the time it passed through me."

184. Which is your favourite incarnation of Lucy Robinson from Neighbours?

Rich says: "I liked the original Lucy best, the William Hartnell Lucy if you will."

185. Do you remember the first time that a childhood enthusiasm was crushed and broken?

Rich says: "I had been at my first disco at Fairlands Middle School and had danced the night away. I was sweating from the exuberance of my movement and went outside. I remember the cold air biting into me, but I didn't care. I was happy. Then Steve Cheeke said, 'You were terrible at dancing.' I have never enjoyed dancing since."

186. What is your favourite archaic word or phrase?

Rich says: "In the middle ages they used to call a skirt 'a fuck-sail'."

187. Who do you consider the most appalling member of Margaret Thatcher's Cabinet (excluding Margaret Thatcher obviously)?

Rich says: "Cecil Parkinson – the way he conducted his personal life was appalling. Though I met him about two weeks before he died and he was avuncular and charming, though broken too."

188. Which is the best small peelable orange-like fruit? The satsuma, the clementine, the mandarin, the tangerine or another small peelable orange-like fruit?

Rich says: "Satsuma"

189. What is your favourite bridge?

190. How many different human beings' poo have you had to deal with?

Rich says: "I think actually only mine and my daughter's… oh no wait, also whoever it was who did a shit by my front gate last year. Probably some others too now I think about it. Oh yeah, I mean if you include THAT, yeah."

191. Which is your favourite bun that is named after a place?

Rich says: "The Chelsea bun is pretty good."

192. If you had to marry a piece of furniture – if you *had* to – which piece of furniture would you marry?

Rich says: "I would marry the Coronation Chair that is in Westminster Abbey, but only if they reinstate the Stone of Scone into the base."

193. Can you describe the most unusual penis you have ever seen?

Rich says: "There is no such thing as a usual penis"

194. Who is the most evil person you have ever met?

Rich says: "I didn't meet him but I once briefly stayed in a hotel room that had just been vacated by President Assad of Syria"

195. When did you feel the most ambivalent?

CAPE BORDA.—*South Australia.*

SOUTH POINT
CAPE OF GOOD HOPE

ROMAN ROCK.—*Cape of Good Hope.*

TROUBRIDGE SHOAL IS-
LAND.—*South Australia.*

BERMUDA.

MOHAJE POINT.—*Jamaica.*

Beacon of wood.—*Cape Race.*

GRAND TURK.—*Bahamas.*

CAPE RACE.—*Newfoundland.*

CAPE PINE.—*Newfoundland.*

196. What does mansplaining mean?

N.B. Ask a man this question and then when he starts explaining shout "Stop mansplaining!" and tut.

197. What is the strangest thing that you've ever found in a fridge?

Rich says: "Milk. I have had a very sheltered life of empty fridges."

198. When you are asked to imagine a time or place when you are calm and happy, what time and/or place do you imagine?

Rich says: "I go back to a holiday I had in Thailand where I was staying in a beach hut and one night at midnight noticed that a small sand-bank had appeared a few metres out to sea. My drunk girlfriend of the time went to bed, but I took a plastic chair and sat on this little island (which I called "Chard Island" after a pretentious shortening of my own first name) and watched the moon crossing the sky."

199. What is your third earliest memory? That is, not your earliest memory or the next earliest one, but the one after that?

200. If you could have a dream dinner party with any person living or dead, who would you employ to do the washing up?

N.B. They would not be allowed to join the dinner party, but would get tantalising snippets of the conversation that always cut off before the interesting bit/punchline.

201. If you dropped your mobile phone down the portaloo on day 3 of the Glastonbury festival, would you retrieve it?

202. If you had the ability to be able to be a virtuoso on any instrument without practising, what instrument would you choose?

203. Do you have a pet peeve? By which I mean is there something that annoys you about your pet?

Rich says: "I didn't like the way that Liono my cat sometimes shat just outside the litter tray – especially when I stood in it."

204. What was the worst occasion in which you were totally naked?

Rich says: "During my play "Excavating Rita" I would be naked every night. It was a humiliating episode for the character I played and the audience usually got it and it was a funny moment, but one time they didn't really react and it felt like I was naked, rather than the character and I was embarrassed. The character then gets punched out and usually I got a cloth thrown over me, but when the actor threw the cloth it missed and so I was lying on the floor with my pathetic genitals on display and unable to do anything to cover myself. I suppose it was my own fault for writing it."

205. Shag, marry or kill? Oxygen, ennui, mitochondria?

204.
What was the worst occasion in which you were totally naked?

206. Would the world be worse or better if every man who said they have a "mancave" was evaporated by a laser?

207. Who are your three favourite ghosts, real or (let's face it) fictional?

Rich says: "Timothy Claypole, Anne Boleyn and the New Shmoo (who I assume is a ghost)."

208. What word are you unable to pronounce out loud?

Rich says: "Opprobrium"

209. What is your favourite colour?

N.B. As they are answering shout, "You're x" where x is whatever their age is. It's kind of funnier if they are 5 actually. And I know I've done that question before, but it still counts because what you have to do is different. If things keep as going badly as this then I think the last 250 questions might all be "What is your favourite colour?"

210. What is the best sound effect you have ever heard?

Rich says: "Without doubt the AIOTM roulette wheel. It's so versatile."

211. Can you name three occasions on which you cheated?

212. If you could turn any one person into a worm, which person would you turn into a worm and why?

213. Where does a bird leave its sexual organs when it goes to a night-club?

Rich says: "In the cloaca room."

214. Would you rather be killed by being shot out of a cannon, dropped into a well or impaled on a giant spike that you have to sit on top of, but you'd very slowly descend on to via your anus?

215. Are you a racist?

N.B. They'll probably say no, but you might catch one out.

216. What is the most expensive thing you ever stole?

217. What is your highest score for one single turn at Scrabble?

Rich says: "I got 212 for "equators" over two triple word scores. If I am honest, I only asked the question so I could show off about it. That's more than most of you will score in a whole game of Scrabble. You idiots."

218. Have you ever seen an angel?

219. Have you ever appeared on a TV quiz show? If so please tell me in excruciating detail about how you got on, especially if you lost...

Rich says: "I have, but I don't like to talk about it."

220. Do you think they will ever make a Hunger Games style film but based around the ITV daytime quiz show, "Tipping Point"?

221. What is the strangest thing you had found in your cleavage, belly button or anal cleft?

222. If you were going to form a barbershop quartet, what would you call it?

223. Would you rather have your brain put in back to front or have your hands and feet swapped round? Because I can arrange to have either done and will do so as soon as you have answered.

224. If you woke up with hands where your feet are and feet where your hands are how quickly do you think you would adapt?

225. Have you planned out what you would do in the event of a zombie apocalypse?

Rich says: "I would hide and wait for the zombies to grind to a halt and rot away. I have a baked bean silo in my house so would not need to leave it for sustenance."

226. Which seemingly respectable celebrity do you suspect is a coked-up sex pest?

Rich says: "REDACTED O' REDACTED"

227. Who would win a fight in a jungle between Muhammed Ali and George Foreman?

Rich says: "Muhammed Ali in the eighth round."

228. What is the least surreal thing you have ever seen?

Rich says: "A fish."

229. What is your favourite Papal name?

Rich says: "Boniface… no Urban… it's so hard to choose."

230. What should be the eighth deadly sin?

Rich says: "Taking up more than your allocated leg room on public transport."

231. Aren't clowns shit?

232. Has anyone you've had sex with, had sex with someone famous?

Rich says: "Yes, everyone who has had sex with me has had sex with me. And I was on "What the Dickens?""

233. If you had to be anally violated by a popular chocolate bar – if you *had* to – which chocolate bar would you like inserted in your anus?

234. After you have been anally violated by the chocolate bar, who would you like to then eat the chocolate bar, not knowing where it had been, whilst you secretly watched them?

235. How much vodka do you have to put into a Bloody Mary before it becomes a Mary?

236. Do you ever think that maybe you are in your own version of the Truman Show?

N.B. If they say "Yes" and start telling you about it as if that's an original thought shout into their faces "Yes, everyone does, you prick. But you're not. So grow up."

237. Isn't liquid soap just an elaborate con?

Rich says: "Yes it is. A bar of soap lasts forever and is more effective at cleaning your hands and you can make it liquid soap by rubbing it under some water."

238. Don't you ever, don't you ever, stop being dandy, showing me you're handsome?

239. Do you think it's acceptable to sit on public transport with your legs akimbo, taking up the people next to you's space?

N.B. If they say "Yes", say, "Well it fucking isn't, so stop doing it!" We'll get to them all eventually.

240. If you had to eat the pants of someone within thirty metres of us – if you *had* to – whose pants would you eat?

N.B. You cannot add sauce to the pants or any kind of topping, other than anything that peels off on to the pants when they are removed.

241. Why won't you ever admit that you are wrong?

242. What is twelve times twelve?

Rich says: "It's 144."

243. Have you ever had a wank in a Jacuzzi (or non-branded hot tub)?

244. What is your favourite direction on a compass?

245. Why don't you wash more?

246. Did you ever forget your games kit and have to do the lesson in stuff from the lost property box?

247. Have you ever tried tilting at windmills?
Rich says: "Yes and the windmills carried on regardless."

248. Have you ever walked through Piccadilly Circus and loudly proclaimed, "Blimey, it's like Piccadilly Circus out here."
Rich says: "Yes, I invented that."

249. What is your favourite kind of non-human milk to drink?
Rich says: "Tasmanian Devil milk is delicious and also helps you fight off superbugs. There'll always be milk."

250. If you could have all your teeth replaced by psychic orbs that could tell you all future events by telepathy, but would scream at a high-pitched volume every time you opened your mouth, would you go ahead with the teeth replacement operation?
N.B. The orbs would be useless for chewing and make your breath smell of sulphur, but you'd win the lottery every week.

251. Would you rather have a clitoris in the crook between your thumb and finger or have a bionic nose?

252. Who is the most inappropriate person you've ever had a sex dream about?

Rich says: "TV's Emma Kennedy, but even in the imaginary dreamscape we could not get aroused by each other's mutually hideous bodies/personalities and it was like stuffing a marshmallow into a letterbox (but not as sexy)."

253. What is the most desperate Emergency Question that you have ever heard or read?

Rich says: "I think so far the tooth/psychic orb one, but to be honest we are only 253 questions in, so I suspect the worst is yet to come."

254. Who do you consider the best of Jesus' disciples?

Rich says: "Thaddeus, because he kept himself to himself and didn't try to stand out by betraying, denying or doubting Jesus. He just believed in him, quietly. Imagine hanging around with Jesus, knowing he was the son of God and then still betraying, denying or doubting him. That would be insane. You witnessed all the miracles and heard all the stuff and must have known that a place in Heaven was guaranteed. So yeah, Thaddeus wins for not being a dick, given all the evidence."

255. What is your favourite memory of being halfway somewhere?

256. Have you ever met your doppelgänger?

257. If your house was on fire what three items would you definitely leave behind, or even surreptitiously throw into the flames when no one was looking?

258. Do you wash your legs when you're having a shower?

259. What is your favourite way to cool down?

260. What's the strangest thing that's ever happened to you in a taxi cab?

261. Have you ever fallen victim to a conman?

Rich says: "Yes, in the mid-90s I was about to move in with my girlfriend, but the estate agent had rented the flat out to 7 or 8 different couples and run off with the deposits. He was eventually caught and we were amazingly reimbursed, but the strain of it all ended the relationship. I think it might have been a lucky escape. I should thank him really."

262. Who can you never forgive?

263. What gives you the right?

264. What has been your least enjoyable experience of food poisoning?

Rich says: "On my birthday in 2010 I woke up feeling bad. I had diarrhoea, but then I realised I was going to vomit and there was no time to flush so had no choice but to vomit on my own diarrhoea. I did this on the hour every hour for the next four hours until I was throwing up bile. It wasn't very pleasant at all. In fact I can't think of a single enjoyable food poisoning story."

265. How do you spell diarrhoea? And why do I have to look it up every time I write it down? And still don't believe that's how you actually spell it even when the dictionary says it is?

266. What age do you think you have to be to be old?

267. What is your highest score in a game of Yahtzee? What do you mean you don't know? What kind of person doesn't know that? An idiot.

Rich says: "Mine is 715, much higher than yours. Even if you don't know it, it still is."

268. Who are you surprised never got Yew-Treed?

Rich says: "REDACTED O' REDACTED"

271.

Why can't we live forever?

269. What is your favourite colour?

N.B. Whatever they say, you say, "Wow, that's my favourite colour too," and then make a look like that's significant before looking lovingly into their eyes. This is a good one to do on a date as if they are stupid they will think it's significant too.

270. Who do you most regret not getting off with when you had the chance?

Rich says: "Bernadette. She was gorgeous and apparently fancied me at college for a couple of weeks and I had no fucking idea. Dick."

271. Why can't we live forever?

272. Do you remember Spangles?

N.B. If the person laughs and says, "YES!" as if that's an original observation then punch them in the face until they bleed.

273. What is the most offensive thing that you can think of?

274. Have you ever been infested? By what exactly?

Rich says: "In my first shared house in London we had a wasps nest in the loft that the landlord dealt with himself by putting plastic bags on his hands and taking it down."

275. Who would win in a fight, King Kong or King Dong?

276. Have you ever taken a lie detector test?

N.B. If they say "No" go "Beeeeep" and say "That's a lie." If they say yes, they probably have quite an interesting story to tell. Sit back and listen.

277. Have you ever done a poo that is so impressive that you've taken a photo so you can show the world? And did you consider sending the picture to the Guinness Book of Records?

278. Which was your favourite McWhirter Twin?

Rich says: "Norris. Though it's like choosing between Hitler and Satan – and I chose Hitler."

279. Would you rather have fingernails made out of 1p pieces or a nostril that could do an uncanny impression of Anne Robinson?

N.B. The 1ps could be taken off and spent as legal tender, but would take a week to grow back. So I am essentially asking if you'd rather have 10p a week or be able to make people think that Anne Robinson was hiding somewhere in the vicinity.

280. Would you rather have an enema or an enemy?

N.B. the enema would be a one off, but the enemy would be for life and very focused on revenge. But would not give you an enema however bad things got.

281. Would you rather have an enema or an anemone?

N.B. the anemone would live on your shower floor and might sting you if you accidentally stood on it.

282. Would you rather have the aforementioned enemy or the aforementioned anemone?

Rich says: "I don't really care. Just glad I came up with something that used up 3 questions. And there's nothing you can do to get your money back. Cheg on, reader, you am a twart!"

283. Do you have a celebrity hand twin?

Rich says: "Yes, the actress Emma Watson has the exact same sized and shaped hands as mine (ie hand-shaped). I am looking for ways to monetise this, but so far it's only been wanking off paedophiles from behind a curtain."

284. What is a more admirable quality: consistence or the ability to change one's mind?

Rich says: "I'd say the latter. The world is fucked cos of all the people who are sure they are right."

285. Which is the best pie? Objectively the best one. I don't want your opinion.

286. What's your favourite fraction?

287. Marmite! Do you love it or hate it? Or don't you mind it? Or have you never tried it? In which case shall we go and buy some so you can try it? OK, got some now. Taste it. Do you love it or hate it or are you ambivalent? Or somewhere on a sliding scale between those points? If so quantify that as a percentage where hate is 0% and love is 100%. Thanks.

288. Which word or phrase do you use but never overuse?

289. Have you ever been brainwashed?

290. Where do you see yourself in 500 years time?

291. If there are ever sex robots, as any right thinking person hopes, would they be self-cleaning? Or would there be another small robot that would clean the sex robot? Or would there be a person whose job was to clean out the sex robot before the next person used it? Can you think of a worse job?

292. Do you think the film *The Flintstones: Viva Rock Vegas* could ever come true?

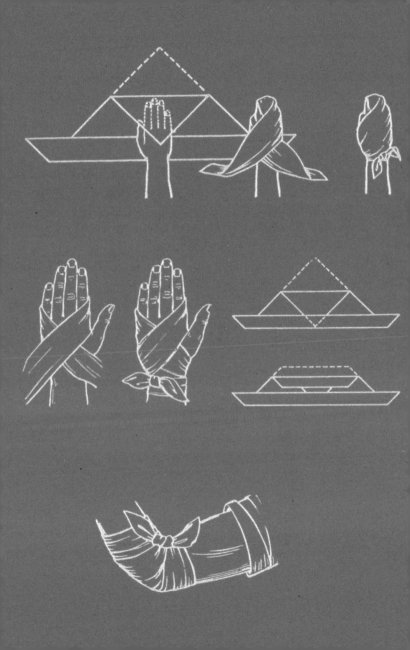

295.

Which is the sexiest TV puppet?

293. What do you think the people of the 22nd Century will find amusing/unbelievable about the people of the 21st Century?

Rich says: "I suspect they will laugh at us killing ourselves with tobacco and sugar in the same way we laugh at the Victorians having lead piping – the idiots."

294. If you had to have sex with Twiki from Buck Rogers or Skippy the Bush Kangaroo – if you *had* to – which one would you have sex with?

295. Which is the sexiest TV puppet?

Rich says: "It's between Janice from the Muppets and Lamb Chop."

296. What is the most libellous thing you can say about Prince Andrew?

297. If they brought back capital punishment would you pull the lever yourself?

298. How many members of Blazing Squad can you name?

N.B. The correct answer is none.

299. What kind of butter/margarine/butter-like spread do you favour?

300. Would you rather have a book with 300 emergency questions in it delivered within two months of the end of a kickstarter campaign or a book with 500 emergency questions delivered about six months after the end of a kickstarter campaign?

Rich says: "What a shame we didn't give you that choice."

301. How much is a pint of bull's semen?

N.B. Remember to Google "What is the current market value of bull's semen?" before you ask this question. It is designed to show whether the person you're asking is in touch with the normal man in the street and buys their own bull's semen or if they send someone out to buy their bull's semen for them.

302. Have you got what it takes to be a steeplejack?

303. What's the funniest thing that's ever happened to you at a funeral?

304. What's your problem with immigrants?

305. What would it take for you to drink a pint of bull's semen?

306. What's the worst hotel that obviously thinks it's a good hotel that you've ever stayed at?

307. Would you like to carry moonbeams home in a jar and if so what would you do with them once you'd got them there? I'm suspicious of your motives.

308. Which ghost of Patrick Swayze would you prefer to encounter: the ghost of Patrick Swayze in Ghost or the ghost of Patrick Swayze in Flashdance?

309. Do you think anyone ever said to Jesus, "God shouldn't play man?"

Rich says: "Dammit, I accidentally wrote a new joke."

310. If Frankie Boyle is the Mick Jagger of comedy: the outspoken voice of the disenfranchised youth, dehumanised and demonised by the press, and feared by parents nationwide – and Dave Gorman is Ringo Starr: an everyman; he's well-known and provides entertainment in a variety of guises, but he still gives the impression he'd be incredibly polite if he ever met your mother then what is Paddy McGuinness?

N.B. Please show your working and do bear in mind that whatever Paddy McGuinness is, it must be what he is in the universe where the other two comedians are how they are described.

311. Do you ever Google yourself or search for yourself on Twitter? What's the worst thing you've seen?

Rich says: "It's all been pretty bad to be honest. Luckily I am aroused by negative criticism and death threats though, so it's all good."

312. Boxer shorts or serendipity?

313. Why hast thou forsaken me?

314. Do you have a preferred ear?

315. What's the most expensive and/or pointless thing that you have bought at auction?

316. Tell me about the most disgusting fart you ever did in public and what repercussions did it have?

317. Do you come from a land down under?

Rich says: "Well yes, we all do, from someone's perspective."

318. How many different chairs (to the nearest seven chairs) have you sat in?

N.B. Whatever they say, say "Wrong!" Because they are. It's way more or less than that.

319. Would you rather have a pituitary gland that gave you a wish every thirteen years or a tap on your knee that gave you limitless cider?

N.B. The pituitary gland does not allow you to wish for cider and also attempts to trick you so that 40% of your wishes backfire in a way that humiliates you and it also doesn't allow you to wish for infinity wishes or that no wishes should humiliate you. Also it doesn't produce iodine so all your hormones are fucked up and you can't wish your way out of it. But you still get 60% good wishes (though not very often). Probably best go for the cider.

320. Would you rather be allergic to wood or not?

Rich says: "Not all the questions are difficult."

321. Would you like to taste my special porridge?

322. Have you ever killed a mouse?

Rich says: "No, but I once threw cumin at one and trapped one underneath the spice rack in my kitchen but was too scared of it to let it out and my flatmate was away all weekend, so I waited til I got home and then he killed it. I was vegetarian at the time. I was a bad vegetarian. But at least I didn't eat the mouse and thus fulfilled the contract of my incorrect beliefs."

323. Would you rather have dandruff that doubled up as an acceptable substitute for ground coriander or smegma that tasted like the most delicious cottage cheese?

324. If I was a carpenter and you were a lady, what carpenting jobs would you get for me and what would be my daily rate?

325. If you had to stick a Borrower up your arse – if you *had* to – which Borrower would you stick up there?

Rich says: "I think Homily Clock's bony nose might provide some anal stimulation. But only if I HAD to."

326. Pizza or ennui?

327. What's your favourite anagram?

Rich says: "Carthorse/Orchestra".

328. What's the most interesting thing that you've done in Ipswich?

Rich says: "Been sick on my own diarrhoea."

329. Would you rather have a computer that automatically wrote 500 emergency questions or a nipple that when tweaked played all of Vivaldi's Four Seasons?

Rich says: "The computer please."

330. Who is the best at getting drunk?

331. Be honest, do you think the quality of these emergency questions is declining or improving as the book goes on?

332. If you had the power to bring about world peace, what would you need weapons manufacturers to give you in order not to use your power?

333. What is the worst Adam Sandler film?

    Rich says: "That's such a hard question. Possibly "I Now Pronounce You Chuck and Larry". But I have a feeling the worst is yet to come.

334. Goodnight Sweetheart is an amazing but flawed sitcom. Could you please give a five-minute speech pointing out some of the flaws?

335. Is there anybody out there?

336. Do you like motorcycling? Motorcycling around? What's your favourite bike?

    Rich says: "I sure do. Rrrum rrrummm. The Kawasaki 792, that's my baby. That's my ride. Rrrrum rrrummmm."

337. What's the best thing you have ever won?

338. When was the last time you cried?

339. Do sperm have dreams?

340. If you could choose any day from your life to have a Groundhog Day on, which day would you choose?

Rich says: "Probably the day at University when I could have got off with Bernadette, but I have a feeling that even if I had the day a billion times I would still mess it up."

341. What's the absolute worst thing about the film Sliding Doors?

Rich says: "It's very hard to choose just one, but it's probably that Gwyneth Paltrow is impressed by a man reciting a Monty Python sketch rather than assuming that he is a douche."

342. How would you feel if you discovered that all your memories were implanted and you are just a robot in a tourist attraction where people pay to interact with you?

N.B. After they give their answer, then say, "Because I am here to tell you that that is in fact the case and I am here to turn you off forever." Then produce a huge screwdriver that looks like it's from an alien civilisation or the future and move towards them with a serious look on your face.

343. What's the strangest thing that has entered your anal canal?

344. Do you have a favourite plate?

Rich says: "Yes I do. I stole it from my college. It has the crest on. It's not a valuable one but I have now had it for nearly 30 years."

345. Have you ever fallen out of a hammock?

Rich says: "Yes I have. I tied up a hammock outside a beach hut in 2001, but I am not very good at knots and I was quite fat and the hammock fell down with me on it. My sweaty skin slapped against the concrete beneath. It hurt me, but falling out of a hammock can never be anything but amusing."

346. What is the most alarming thing that has entered or exited your body?

347. Which actor (male or female) do you think would make the worst James Bond?

Rich says: "CJ from Eggheads."

348. Desert Island Dirks: If you were stranded on a desert island, but were able to take eight Dirks with you, which eight Dirks would you take?

Rich says: "Dirk Bogarde, obviously, Radio Producer Dirk Maggs, Dirk Benedict from the A Team, Dirk Diggler, Dirk Hillbrecht, Dirk Kuyt, Dirk Blocker and Dirk Gently."

349. If you had to choose between killing all of the Eggheads or all of the Chasers on the Chase – if you *had* to – which group of quiz nerds would die?

Rich says: "Definitely the Eggheads. Firstly, Chaser Paul "The Sinhaman" Sinha is a friend of mine, but also no member of the Chasers (as far as I know) has ever said they have kicked someone into a canal and might have killed them. So even though there are more Eggheads, I feel that more people are likely to die if the Eggheads reign of terror is allowed to continue."

350. What do you think Ben Shepherd really feels about presenting Tipping Point?

351. Have you ever sucked on a fisherman's friend (lower case)?

352. If you had to give cunnilingus to a fish – if you had to – which fish would you lick out?

Rich says: "A mermaid. Even though it would be exactly the same as giving cunnilingus to a fish (I imagine) I could look up and see a lady and wouldn't feel so bad. If that's not allowed then it would have to be a halibut, the fish with the sexiest vagina – I am guessing"

353. Have you ever been in the vicinity of a celebrity when they have farted? How was it?

354. Can you name a solo artist that had a number one in the 1980s that would have scored under 7 points on Pointless?

Rich says: "Yes, I can now."

355. Have you ever gone chasing waterfalls?

Rich says: "No, I have stuck to chasing the rivers and lakes that I am used to. Though chasing a lake is really easy."

356. How many roads must a man walk down before you can call him a man?

Rich says: "11 roads."

357. Why do they call the place you put your fresh bread, a bread bin? And what do they call the place where you dispose of your non-fresh bread?

358. Have you ever been possessed by a demon? Or been accused of being a demon? And are you a demon?

I think you're a demon.

359. Have you ever pretended to be your own twin (whether you have one or not)?

360. What is the worst song by the Red Hot Chilli Peppers?

N.B. It's a trick question. It's all of them. And they are all the same song anyway.

361. What is the most unusual thing that you've ever used as a toilet paper substitute?

Rich says: "My grandparents used to use that greaseproof medical toilet paper which is as unlike toilet paper as it's possible for a piece of toilet-paper shaped paper to be."

362. Where did your family go on holiday when you were a child?

Rich says: "The Isle of Arran. I remember that it rained a lot. And we had a real fire. One time my dad let me sit on his knee and steer the car and I nearly drove us off the road. I was 28 years old."

363. Who would you place in the inner circle of Hell?

Rich says: "As trite as it is to say a politician, I believe David Cameron has done more to be responsible for fucking up our future than anyone else. I hope he is right in Satan's pants."

364. Could you live without the Internet? Because if you say you can't, you fucking can.

365. Do you remember the first time you were stung by a bee or a wasp or some similar yellow and black, striped, flying, stinging insect?

Rich says: "Of course I do. No one could forget that sharp and unwarranted pain. It was summer and I was by some water and wearing no shirt and I brought my arm down as a wasp or bee or some other flying, stinging insect was in the vicinity and it stung me right in the armpit. I wonder if that is the psychological reason why I want sun cream to come from there. To soothe me."

366. If I gave you £4000 would you put a cumpkin on your head? If not £4000, then how much would it take for you to lower a jack a lantern filled with the ejaculant of 5 men over your hair and face? Damn, would you have done it for less than £4000?

367. Which is preferable: starch or ambiguity?

368. Would you rather be an orchestra that has been assimilated by the Borg and endlessly plays only orchestral versions of Mel and Kim songs or a carthorse that has to pull a cart full of the corpses of all your carthorse friends around all day long, but is otherwise treated well and gets Sunday off?

369. Can you smell that?

N.B. If you sniff during this to suggest you can smell something, they will try and smell it too and you can have a lively conversation about what the non-existent smell is.

370. How cracked/broken does a mug have to be before you throw it away?

Rich says: "Only if it is actively leaking liquid or smashed to the point where it can't even hold liquid. It can lose its handle and be chipped to buggery, but if I can still drink out of it, providing bits of mug aren't falling into my drink, then it's safe."

371. Can you believe you read this far? Or are you just dipping in?

372. Do you have what it takes to be a berserker?

373. If you could be any character in William "Ringpiece" Thackeray's *Vanity Fair*, which character would you be? What do you mean you haven't read it? Go on read it. I will wait here for you to finish and then come back and tell me. NO, you CAN'T just watch the film.

374. When you were a child did you have an imaginary friend?

375. How would you say human life would be improved if, like birds and lizards we had a cloaca instead of our sexual/urinary organs and anuses?

Rich says: "It would be better all round, but principally every time you had sex you'd be having vaginal and anal. Which would make you a winner. A cloaca-fucking winner."
Interesting fact: Cloaca is Latin for sewer.

376. Have you ever been to the toilet at the same time as Benedict Cumberbatch?

Rich says: "Yes I have and furthermore it was in a toilet in Buckingham Palace. He had finished his business though, so I didn't get to see his junk. But I imagine, like him, it resembles an otter."

377. If you had to swap your sexual organs for an animal (not the sexual organs of the animal, but the entire animal) – if you *had* to – which animal would you swap with?

378. What is your favourite punchline?

Rich says: "Lemon entry, my dear Watson."

379. If you could Kickstart anything, what would it be?

Rich says: "A motorcycle, cos I sure love motorcycling. Rrrrummm rrrrummmm."

380. Oh come off it, I was clearly referring to the popular crowdfunding website. Any ideas for that?

Rich says: "I can't really see that ever working."

381. What do women want?

382. What did the smelliest cab driver you've ever been in a taxi with smell of?

Rich says: "He's not the smelliest, but the one I am in a cab with now smells very heavily of cigarettes. Like he's been bathing in butts."

383. Have you ever been in a police car?

Rich says: "I have. When I had my mobile phone stolen out of my hand by a man on a bicycle, the police whizzed me round Shepherd's Bush Green to look for him. I had a Hitler Moustache at the time, which is, I assume, why the police were so keen to help."

384. What's the strangest statue you've ever seen?

Rich says: "It's a toss up between the "Pesticles" statue on Hammersmith roundabout, where three men crouch or stand up with strange combined penis and testicle genitals (pesticles) meaning that when viewed through Starbucks window one of them looks like he is doing a shit. Or otherwise it's the statue of a modern day man meeting Abraham Lincoln in the town centre of Warsaw, Indiana and looking more surprised by the President's hat than the appearance of the President."

385. What is the most unlikely thing you've ever done on a bus?

N.B. You can tell your anecdote as a joke at a later date. Tell the anecdote without revealing you are on a bus and then say "And then I got off the bus!" Come up with six of those and you can be a professional comedian.

386. Why did Itsu in Notting Hill change from a sit down sushi restaurant with all the stuff going round on a conveyor belt to just selling stuff out of fridges? Well, can you find out please?

387. And now it's the extra special Caitlin Moran emergency question: "Have you ever pooed in a bag?"

Rich says: "No, I haven't, but a girlfriend of mine once weed in a carrier bag in the car when we were in a traffic jam."

388. Why did Jesus say, "Why Hast Thou Forsaken Me?" on the cross? Had he forgotten about the plan that He and His Dad had come up with to save mankind?

389. Which of the thousands of gods in (possibly imaginary) existence is the most ludicrous? Feel free to make one up if you can't think of an "actual" one.

390. Have you ever seen a UFO or an alien outside of a UFO or an alien beaming into a UFO or running up the gang-plank of a UFO?

391. Have you ever seen the band UFO?

392. Have you ever seen the band UFO in a UFO or running up the gang-plank of a UFO?

393. Which toy did you always want for Christmas, but never received? When you were an adult did you buy it for yourself and if so was it as good as you had hoped?

Rich says: "I always wanted Scalextric. But I never got it. My wife bought me some a few years back. I found it a bit childish to be honest."

394. What is your favourite collar?

N.B. If they start telling you their favourite colour, shout in their face, "I said COLLAR, you idiot."

395. If you had to permanently seal up one of the holes in your body (I am not including the pores in your skin or hair follicles so don't be a smart arse) – if you *had* to – which hole would you permanently seal up and why? And what would the repercussions be?

396. If Abraham Lincoln materialised in front of you, having travelled from the past and you had 45 seconds to converse with him, what would you say? Or would you just stare at his hat?

397. Have you ever been somewhere foreign and obscure and unexpectedly bumped into someone you know?

Rich says: "Yes, I once met a comedy promoter from London on a beach in a not very touristy part of Thailand. What of it?"

398. Are there more questions than answers? What if you include wrong answers?

Rich says: "Shit, I've accidentally written another joke."

399. Can you answer this question with a question?

400. What is the least amazing coincidence that you have ever experienced?

401. Do you believe in life after love? Because if not there is something badly wrong with you and you should see a brain doctor.

402. Have you ever met a shepherd?

403. If you could be shrunk down and somehow be able to go on a Fantastic Voyage inside your own body (why accept the first part and not the second?), what part of your internal body would you go to explore?

N.B. You only have time to look round one organ/gland or whatever and if you stay inside too long you will return to normal size and then blow your own body apart and as your body will now be in two realities that will create a tear in the fabric of the universe that will destroy everything, so please be punctual with your exit.

404. How late are you prepared to stay up to get lucky?

Rich says: "Certainly not all night, that's insane. You'll be left with the dregs and everyone will be too tired to do anything. Personally if I haven't got lucky by 10.30pm then I am off home. I might stay up to midnight if there was a strong hint that I was going to get lucky in those extra 90 minutes. But I'd be really annoyed if I failed to get lucky after that additional effort as I'd probably have to get a cab or a night bus."

405. How can you be sure of anything?

406. To be or not to be?

Rich says: "To be. Obviously. Shit question. Who thought that one up?"

407. Who is your favourite Julian?

Rich says: "Julian Dutton who played the Canon Man in the early 1990s."

408. What is your favourite memory of Stuart Maconie remembering something?

409. Have you ever seen a starling?

Rich says: "I mean, almost certainly, but not knowingly."

410. What children's toy or accessory do you wish they did in adult size?

Rich says: "Almost all of them, but I would love to go on an adult-sized version of soft play. I bet that exists somewhere. Also I wouldn't mind being pushed around in a pram all the time and shitting in a nappy and having someone have to clean my arse for me. I am certain that service is available."

411. Would you rather be able to turn your head like an owl or have a neck that telescopes up to the length of a giraffe's neck (but can go back down to normal neck length at will)?

412. What was the biggest lie your parents ever told you?

413. What is the most expensive thing you ever lost?

414. Would you rather be in Right Said Fred or ZZ Top?

Rich says: "Always go with the beards."

415. What part of you goes the reddest?

416. Who is your favourite Plantagenet? If you don't know what that is you are allowed to say your favourite plant or planet, but will look stupid, especially if you can't think of one.

Rich says: "Edward I, because he killed Mel Gibson."

417. What do you imagine it's like being Stephen Fry?

418. If you had to drink the entire contents of a well-stocked sperm bank or be placed in a coma for ten years where everyone thinks you're not conscious but you can actually hear and feel everything – if you *had* to – which option would you take?

Rich says: "I'd drink the spunk. You'd be doing a fair amount of that in the coma I'd warrant anyway."

419. Have you ever made an actual life decision based on numerology or astrology or any of the bullshit -ologies? How did it turn out?

420. What's the strangest thing that has happened to you or that you've seen in a Post Office?

421. What do you consider to be the most impressive achievement of Simon de Montford?

Rich says: "That they named Leicester Poly after him."

422. How do you pronounce scone?

Rich says: "I pronounce it the only correct way – scone. Anyone who says scone is a fucking idiot."

423. What is the highest number that you've ever successfully counted up to from 1?

424. If your view on religion turned out to be wrong, which belief system would be your second choice?

Rich says: "I wouldn't mind a crack at being Amish."

425. Do you remember Barnaby the Bear?

Rich says: "Yes I do, but I might be the only one. "Barnaby the Bear's my name, never call me Jack or James, I will sing my way to fame, cos Barnaby the Bear's my name. La la lala laaah, la la la la lah lah laaaa" and so on. I bet even fewer people remember Rocket Robin Hood though. Just me and my mate Phil Fry, "Band of Brothers, marching together, heads held high in all kinds of weather…." And so on. This is why I am not Peter Kay."

426. What if God was one of us?

Rich says: "It would make no odds, would it? Unless he told us."

427. What's the best thing you ever found down the back of a sofa?

428. Do you have an heirloom?

429. Would you rather have an elbow made out of marshmallow or a foot that transformed into a were-foot every full moon?

N.B. No more explanation required.

430. If there was a TV quiz show with four contestants, where the first prize was 10 million pounds, but if you came last you were publicly executed, would you go on it? Also second prize is a holiday in Portugal and third prize is a £10 gift token.

431. What's the most bizarre thing that's happened to you when you have been on drugs?

Rich says: "When I took magic mushrooms at Glastonbury I saw the devil masturbating with some liver (it turned out to be a guy stroking his girlfriend's arm). Also the sky became the sea and it was like I was in the sky looking down at it. That was actually quite cool. Drugs are awesome. Take them all now."

432. Have you ever considered writing a poetry book for young adults?

433. What's the worst thing you've eaten for a bet?

Rich says: "At a party I said I would eat a whole pack of butter for £50. I only got two bites in. It was rank. How could something so delicious be so awful? It's almost like you can have too much of a good thing."

434. Which do you prefer, sudokus or kakuros?

Rich says: "I much prefer kakuros, and don't understand why the Guardian only has one a week, when it has a sudoku every day! Come off it. Kakuros are the best. Sure, not so many people have heard of them, but that doesn't mean anything."

435. Would you rather have an immortal goose that laid one golden egg every fifty years and you didn't know when it laid its last golden egg (and it never laid normal eggs) or a mortal goose that would lay a regular egg every day guaranteed, but due to goose illnesses and short life span might die at any time (but also might live for however long an old goose lives)?

N.B. The upkeep of both geese is the same and costs less than the price of a goose egg per day.

436. If you had a finger that could cure rectal cancer, but only if you pushed it hard up the anus of the cancer sufferer, would you cure anyone, everyone or be like Jesus and just cure a few?

437. What is your favourite colour?

N.B. Whatever they say, shout "RACIST!" at them and then storm out looking affronted and never speak to them again, even if they are your partner or parent.

438. What's the most surprising thing or person that has ever leapt out at you?

439. Are you now or have you ever been a member of the Communist Party of the United States?

N.B. If they say "No", say, "Well you would say that."

440. If you had to invent a fifth season, which two other seasons would you put it between and what would happen during it?

441. If you could swap a TV show that went on for too long with one that was cancelled too soon (i.e. the series that was cancelled would get the extra series), which shows would you choose?

Rich says: "I would give the last four series of *Last of the Summer Wine* to get four more series of *Freaks and Geeks*."

442. Why is there a Mr Potato Head but no Mr Tomato Bollocks?

443. If you could be any character in the Simpsons, how would you cope with the fact that you were fictional and only spoke or did anything at the whim of writers and animators?

444. What was the funniest prank call that you ever made?

Rich says: "Once me and my friends found someone called Andrew Belcher in the phone book and rang him up and said, "Hello, is A Belcher there?" He said that he was A Belcher and we laughed and he said, "Oh, very funny" in a sarcastic voice. 28 years old we were."

445. Would you rather have a mirror in which you could see all your dead relatives and friends, but not be able to talk to them, but see them sadly waving at you or a voucher for two for one pizza at Pizza Express (Monday through Thursday)?

446. Which TV personality are you most surprised has got a job because they are so bad at what they do and makes you suspect that they have slept or are sleeping with the right person?

Rich says: "I don't know about the sex part, but I can't believe Jacob Scipio who hosts the Cbeebies show Kerwhizz is on TV. He is so bad at this show that it looks like he's playing a character of a bad TV presenter in a sketch. Also he is very good looking."

447. Biscuits or actresses?

448. If you could live in any era, why did you choose this one?

449. If you only had a week to live, who would you tell to go fuck themselves?

450. If you had to eat a person – if you *had* to – who would you eat and in what order would you devour their body sections?

451. If your lovemaking can be described by a weather event or a natural disaster, what would it be?

   Rich says: "An April Shower."

452. Would you rather have pubic hair made of unremovable barbed wire or to be attacked by a rabid badger in your sleep once a week?

453. Can you knit? What's the best thing you ever knitted?

454. Do you think thunderstorms were invented by NASA to muffle the sound of space battles?

455. Did you have a sticker album or collect PG Tips cards as a child? Can you still remember the cards/stickers you never found?

Rich says: "I don't think I ever found the big green caterpillar from "The Wonders of Wildlife" PG Tips collection. If anyone has it please let me know, but also I will need all the others too as I don't know where I put my album."

456. What was your favourite Kinder Egg Toy?

Rich says: "'The Crazy Crocos' is objectively the correct answer to this question. Accept no other answer and do not move on until the person you are asking has acknowledged this. Even if they don't know what Kinder eggs are and have never heard of Crazy Crocos. You are not allowed to prompt them either, they will have to keep guessing until they come up with this answer."

457. How many weeks would you have to attend Roman Catholic Holy Communion before you had eaten an entire Jesus? Please show your working.

458. How much time do you spend on the toilet when you are doing a poo?

Rich says: "Ages. I wrote this question while doing a poo. That's what gave me the idea. But I bet you can learn a lot about someone's personality from whether they dump and go or enjoy wallowing in their smelly chamber of solitude."

457. HOW MANY WEEKS WOULD YOU HAVE TO ATTEND ROMAN CATHOLIC HOLY COMMUNION BEFORE YOU HAD EATEN AN ENTIRE JESUS?

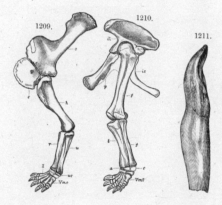

1209.   1210.   1211.

459. Do you have a favourite dinosaur?
No, I don't mean species of dinosaur, I mean individual actual (not fictional) dinosaur. What was his or her name?

460. Would you rather be lactose intolerant or the Prime Minister of the Central African Republic?

Rich says: "I'd really hate not to be able to drink the milk of all the animals, but it would be a big upheaval to move to Africa and I'd feel bad for taking Simplice Sarandji's job. I think I'd just be lactose intolerant and still drink the milk and take the consequences."

461. Would you prefer to have lungs that turned oxygen into jam that would come out of the pores of your skin and could be scraped into bottles and sold (as long as you didn't tell your customers where it was coming from) or an anus that weeped Manuka honey (which could also be sold, though imagine the anger if people found out where you'd been getting that sweet, sweet honey)?

462. Would you rather have a hand made out of ham or a finger that could travel through time?

463. Would you rather have an armpit that dispenses suncream or a nipple that produces talcum powder?

464. Would you rather have an armpit that dispenses talcum powder or a nipple that produces suncream?

465. Would you be annoyed if the rest of the book was just subtle variations on the same basic question?

466. Have you ever been on a plane that's been in an emergency and seen a genuine look of fear on the face of a flight attendant?

Rich says: "Yes, I was once on a plane that started filling up with smoke and had to fly to the nearest airport. I was drunk and missed the announcement about what was happening so had no idea how serious things were. Until I saw the lady who'd been serving me gin and tonics looking properly frightened. I remained calm throughout. Even when the fire engines were running alongside the plane as it landed. Don't worry, I wasn't killed."

467. What type of vacuum cleaner do you use? Do you have a dream vacuum cleaner that you aspire to own one day?

468. Have you ever seen someone passing you and then shortly after seen the same person passing you and rather than assuming they are twins, thought that maybe there was a glitch in the Matrix and done a literal double-take to check?

Rich says: "Funny you should ask. That happened to me last week. I saw a cartoonish middle-aged man on a mobility scooter, with cuddly toys and flags and brightly coloured clothes who waved at me. Seconds later I saw the exact same thing and the twin explanation only came to me when I had confirmed I could see him twice."

469. Is there a race of people who you secretly believe should be exterminated in death camps?

N.B. That's another trick one designed to draw out concealed racism.

470. Which change in name of a popular product most annoyed you?

Rich says: "I didn't like it when they changed Olivio to Bertolli, because I had a routine about how someone had thought I had declared my love for them, rather than suggesting a topping for toast. But in the end it made it better because I claimed they changed the name because too many people were being forced into long term relationships. Arthur Smith has a similar problem with his joke about entering a Marathon. But he just kept doing it and complained that it had been ruined by the name change. So Opal Fruits."

471. Have you ever watched something on Facebook Live that hasn't been totally shit?

472. Have you ever seen a Frankingstein in real life?

473. What is the most public place that you have ever given or received oral sex?

474. What thing do you fear the least?

Rich says: "Actually a tough question. Because a surprising number of innocuous things can hurt you. I was going to say cheese, but if that's off it can give you food poisoning, then I thought a flannel but that can harbour germs. My own ear was my next thought, but what if it got cancer and killed me? I don't know? I have nothing to not fear except a lack of fear itself."

475. What is your most appealing habit?

476. If you could edit your past would you refuse to do so because of the terrible domino effects changing even one thing could have? Or would you take the gamble that erasing one of your errors might be better for the world in general?

477. What swear word would you like repeatedly shouted by a drunk man at your funeral? The drunk man is turning up regardless. And is going to shout something. So you might as well choose.

478. If you had to have sex with either Zippy, Bungle, George, Geoffrey or Rod (whilst Jane and Freddy had sex with each other next to you, but you couldn't join in) – if you *had* to – which of the Rainbow crew would you have sex with?

479. If you didn't have to have sex with either Zippy, Bungle, George, Geoffrey or Rod (but not Jane or Freddy who would now be asleep) but they all said they were up for it if you fancied it, but not an orgy situation, it would have to be one-on-one, would you have sex with one of them and which one?

480. If you had the choice between ending all war or personally receiving £10 million (but war would continue as before), which would you choose?

481. Is it OK to feel a bit sorry for Justin Lee Collins?

482. Is "Improvisation My Dear Mark Watson" the worst title for a TV show ever or can you think of a worse one?

483. Do you think Toy Story 2 could ever happen in real life?

484. Are you able to prove to me that Walter Raleigh and Francis Drake are not actually the same person?

485. If you could choose anyone to be your parents, who would you choose?

Rich says: "Michael Palin and my actual mum. Sorry Dad."

486. What's the most terrifying encounter that you've ever had with a ventriloquist dummy?

Rich says: "Probably when Stewart Lee tried to wank me off using the hand of a hundred year old dummy made by my own great-grandad. Probably."

487. What would be your favourite choice of animal to evolve to take over the world and make humans their slaves, like in Planet of the Apes, but with it not being apes, but the animal you said instead?

Rich says: "I'd like Planet of the Okapis. No problem with being slaves to them at all."

488. If you were looking round a house and thinking of buying it, would it put you off if there was a life size robot made out of toasters in the lounge? Just asking for a friend.

489. If you had to live out the rest of your life being either Toby Young or Dom Joly – if you *had* to – would you just kill yourself now?

490. When I needed a neighbour were you there, were you there? When I needed a neighbour were you there?

Rich says: "No, I wasn't there."

491. I was hungry and thirsty were you there, were you there, I was hungry and thirsty were you there?

Rich says: "No, I wasn't there."

492. I was cold, I was naked were you there, were you there? I was cold I was naked, were you there?

Rich says: "Yes, on that occasion I was there. But I apologised and destroyed the polaroids and we said we'd never talk about this again."

493. Have you ever refused to dance in the rain whilst all your friends are doing it, because you think they're stupid?

Rich says: "Yes and I regret it. It is a metaphor for my existence."

494. Do you think if you do something long enough,
however unfunny it might actually be, that
it will become the most hysterical thing that
you've ever seen?

Rich says: "I don't know, but let's hope so."

495. Does sex with a robot count as cheating, if the
robot is an exact copy of your partner in looks
and personality? Or is that actually the greatest
compliment you can give to your partner? And
also the biggest waste of making a sex robot
ever. How about if the robot is an exact copy of
what your partner looked like when you first
met them? Amazing how things can turn on a
sixpence, isn't it?

496. Do you think you have cried more tears or
created more sexual juices in your lifetime
and would you appreciate some afterlife
It's A Knockout dipstick affair to settle the
question in Heaven?

N.B. If 1000 people sign a petition to request that then God has to
institute it .

497. What is the most embarrassing injury you've ever had?

Rich says: "I was knocked over by a wave in Barbados, hit my head in the shallow water and for some reason one of my testicles swelled to about four times its (already impressive) size. It also acted as quite an accurate altimeter on the way home on the plane, hurting more as the plane got higher."

498. Have you ever written something fictional that then came true in real life?

Rich says: "So many things that I think I might be magic. I went out with Julia Sawalha for God's sake. After all that shrine malarkey. And that's just the start of it."

499. If Newton's Laws of Motion is true then how come there are still monkeys?

500. What's the stupidest thing you've done for no money?

Rich says: "Spending days of precious work time writing this book when I had proper paid work to do. It's been stupid, but I've loved every minute. Thanks for reading it."

BONUS QUESTIONS

Just in case I've miscounted, which I almost certainly have, or done the same question twice, (again highly likely, but like Ben Elton I don't believe in second drafts or proofreading) here's some free ones.

501. What is it that makes us so fear silence that we feel the need to ask ridiculous and pointless questions in order to avoid it?

502. Have you been to Nando's before?

503. What is your favourite Biblical place name?

504. Where did it all go wrong?

505. How would you escape from a Nazi prisoner of war camp?

506. Is it really possible to dress up in a costume that is too distasteful at Halloween or isn't that kind of the whole point?

507. Why can't we all just be friends?

508. If I am born a bigot, does anyone have a right to tell me that my lifestyle choice is wrong and I should change and be like them?

509. Have you ever falsely accused anyone of witchcraft?

510. Have you ever correctly accused anyone of witchcraft?

511. Did the real witch take their revenge on you?

512. Am I alone in thinking it's highly unlikely you not only met a witch but also were brave enough to accuse them?

513. Would you rather live in the waxy ear of a grumpy giant, eating only what flies in there by accident and not being able to make a noise for fear of being ejected with a huge cotton bud or live in Middlesbrough?

514. Whodunit?

515. Will you please tell your friend to buy this book?

507.

Why can't we all just be friends?

Please write your own Emergency Questions here.........

516.

EMERGENCY QUESTIONS

EMERGENCY QUESTIONS